VISIONS: THE ART OF BEV DOOLITTLE

A Catalogue of Published Works

VISIONS: THE ART OF BEV DOOLITTLE

TEXT BY JUDITH HOHL AND
BEV DOOLITTLE

THE GREENWICH WORKSHOP

"I want to change the experience of seeing... to have people think when they look at my paintings."
– B E V   D O O L I T T L E

Frontispiece illustration: sketches from "Woodland Encounter"

© 1988 The Greenwich Workshop, Inc.

ISBN 0-86713-005-9
Library of Congress Catalog Card Number: 88-080892
Design by Peter Landa
Printed by The Columbia Printing Company, Inc.
Bound by Hartford Bindery, Inc.
Stock from Lindenmeyr and Butler Paper Companies
Typography by Typographic Art, Inc.

Printed in the U.S.A.

FOREWORD

I FIRST HEARD of Bev Doolittle in 1978 when a friend told me of an extraordinary work by a new California artist on exhibit at the American Watercolor Society in New York City.

Intrigued by his enthusiasm, I decided to see it for myself. The painting was *Pintos*, the artist, Bev Doolittle. I was so taken with her talent and the uniqueness of her vision that I called her at her home in California about publishing *Pintos* as a limited edition print. The rest is history.

Pintos was issued in 1979 as Bev Doolittle's first limited edition and upon release was sold out, a phenomenon unheard of for a new artist and a first-time print.

Since that time, The Greenwich Workshop has had the pleasure of working with Bev in publishing twenty-one limited edition prints, a limited edition book and a poster. We have enjoyed working with her and sharing in the enthusiasm which underlies all her work.

We look forward to the years to come and travelling down whatever paths Bev Doolittle's magic takes us.

DAVID P. USHER
President, The Greenwich Workshop

THE BEV DOOLITTLE PHENOMENON

BEV DOOLITTLE'S first print, *Pintos*, was published in a limited edition of 1,000 in 1979.

Nine short years later, collector demand for her work has skyrocketed; her latest personal commission (subscription) print, *Season of the Eagle*, has broken all records in the limited edition print world with an edition size of 36,548.

Since that first introduction in 1979, The Greenwich Workshop has offered Bev Doolittle's work to a growing, enthusiastic audience of collectors. Not only did each published limited edition sell out on release, but collector demand has also created an astounding secondary (resale) market with some prints selling as much as 3000% to 4000% over issue price.

Bev Doolittle's rare original works are avidly sought by collectors. Each takes months of research, preparation and painting in the demanding medium of transparent watercolor before completion and she creates only two to three works a year. These originals command up to $75,000.

What lies behind this extraordinary phenomenon? The answer is simple — it is the unique vision and the very special talent of Bev Doolittle. A vision and a talent that have created the most coveted limited edition prints today; images that will be appreciated for generations to come.

Bev Doolittle's work is so unique that it has caught the attention of such diverse media as *Southwest Art*, *Collector Editions*, *Midwest Art*, *Prints*, *Western Art Digest*, *Ranger Rick*, and *The National Enquirer* as well as television networks throughout North America.

Doolittle's art speaks to many people on many levels, ranging from a 4th grade program themed "Hidden Worlds" to a college textbook on the psychology of perception.

Her art has gathered accolades from galleries who offer her work, from art critics and enthusiasts, and from collectors throughout the world:

"When looking upon Bev Doolittle's works, you are drawn into another world, another place, another time, when everything was a story and every story an adventure."
– Dan Smith, Art Director, *National Wildlife*

"Bev Doolittle masterfully blends imagination and a moment of life in her paintings. If the viewer isn't careful, the detail and subtle interplay of setting and subject could be overlooked. But who would want to miss it?"
– Robert Koenke, Publisher, *Wildlife Art News*

"We featured Bev's work on one of our issues – it sold more copies and sold faster than any issue we've ever published. Her work is fantastic, unique, painstaking, playful and gaining admirers all the time."
– Paul Froiland, Editor, *U.S. Art*

"In the tradition of Frederic Remington and Charles Russell but with a style all her own, Bev Doolittle breathes new life into Western Americana. The collection of her works will assure that she attains her rightful place among the great portrayers of the West."
– Gregg R. Oehler, Publisher, Empire Press

"We've had an extraordinary response to her art, mainly from older readers and their parents who have loved her work. I don't know of any art we've published lately that has generated this kind of response."
– Gerry Bishop, Editor, *Ranger Rick*

"I love Bev Doolittle's work. I wish I had more walls."
– Janet Pepper, Los Angeles, California

"Bev Doolittle paints with her heart and mind as well as her hand. Bev Doolittle gives us pleasures that never grow old or fade with time."
– Ed and Hap Scovel, Essex, Connecticut

"We find peace in her images which reflect a harmony between man and nature often overlooked in our world."
– Edie and Sam Anderson, Westport, Connecticut

"Each release is based on a different theme with a unique quality that sets it apart from not only other artists' work, but from her own. The phrase 'if you've seen one, you've seen them all' never applies when speaking of Bev Doolittle's work."
– Brian Millis, Gallery Alaska Anchorage, Alaska

"Bev Doolittle's works have a magical quality that attracts people to them like a magnet. She is truly one of a kind."
– Dan and Pat Howard, Howard/Mandville Gallery Edmonds, Washington

"Bev's work is outstanding and unique. Her images sell themselves and have collectors begging for more."
– Alan Brown, Gallery One, Mentor, Ohio

"The art of Bev Doolittle opens not only our eyes but our minds to new vistas through her unique creativity. The response to her work is both awe (how did she do it?) and delight. Our collectors eagerly await each future print, anxiously wanting to know what she is doing next."
Gail and Bearl Coulter, Gailco Galleries Chattanooga, Tennessee

"Bev's work is so clever and completely unique that new people discover it for the first time with each release. New prints come out every day in this industry and there's always a few people who will say 'that's nice.' When a new Bev Doolittle print comes out, people pay attention; it's an event."
– Bob Brown, Big Horn Gallery, Cody, Wyoming

"Bev Doolittle's art meets not only the eye, but also challenges our ability to perceive beyond the surface of a colored image. Her work is like good reading, witty, imaginative, suspenseful and poetic."
– Bernadette Johnson, Bernadette's North Vancouver, B.C. Canada

"Bev Doolittle collectors buy her work because it brings them to a time when the country was unspoiled and full of wonder and mystery. Her works take the viewer back to that precious time and show them the spirit of the people and the wildlife. The admirer explores her art, experiences glimpses of the unknown and a world gone by, but which is still a part of each and every one of us. She keeps the magic alive in each new work she creates."
– Vivian Raisch, John Lane Gallery Poughkeepsie, New York

THE ART OF BEV DOOLITTLE

THE ART OF BEV DOOLITTLE encompasses the whimsical, the mystical and spiritual, and her own unique camouflage concepts. These themes are interwoven within the complete body of her work and each reveals a different aspect of the artist herself.

Her style is characterized by meticulous realism, unsparing attention to detail and an extraordinary talent for drawing. Many of her works are narrative, telling a story or capturing a moment in the world of dreams or the realm of the spirit. Her storytelling captures the imagination, compelling the viewer to bring his own understanding to the work.

Her whimsical works, like *Bugged Bear, Escape by a Hare,* and *Whoo?!* are commentaries on life in the wild. They show Doolittle's basic love of nature and evoke in us a vision of the world seen through the animal's eyes. Doolittle's special gift draws us into this world of nature and allows us to share in the magic she creates.

The large group of her works dealing with the spirit world focus on the life of the American Indian in the West of a hundred years ago. They show not just the myths and legends of the Indian, but they capture the spiritual world that was the very essence of his existence.

In a world full of danger and uncertainty, the Indian identified with and relied on the strength and power of a vision-inspired animal totem, be it the grizzly, wolf, eagle or other animal. Surrounding himself with the emblems of their power, as in *Guardian Spirits,* he possessed their peculiar attributes himself. He became one with the spirit protector(s), looked to them for his strength and ordered his life by the signs they gave him.

In such works as *Spirit of the Grizzly, Eagle's Flight, Rushing War Eagle, Runs with Thunder, Wolves of the Crow, Two Bears of the Blackfeet* and *Calling the Buffalo,* Doolittle opens the door to the world of the spirit and leads us to an understanding of the forces at work there. In *The Good Omen* and *Let My Spirit Soar,* we, too, can hear the whispers of the spirit and sense the goodness they bring.

Doolittle's ability to invoke the spiritual aspects of nature is seen in *Unknown Presence* and *Christmas Day, Give or Take a Week.* Man appears almost insignificant in the vastness of nature, whether in the enveloping dark of night or in the cathedral presence of giant sequoias.

The most popular and intriguing body of work created by Bev Doolittle is her unique camouflage art. In each image, she focuses our attention on a recognizable scene. The titles of the works hint that more is happening than what we first see. We discover an image within an image.

Bev Doolittle's unique and intricately constructed camouflage art; *Pintos, Woodland Encounter, The Forest Has Eyes, Two Indian Horses, Missed, Season of the Eagle* and *Doubled Back;* is executed with skill and imagination. It demands our attention and compels our involvement and our appreciation.

THE ARTIST

"BEV LITERALLY COULD DRAW as soon as she picked up a pencil," says her mother. "Even before she went to school, she had started drawing horses and people." Bev won her first award at age twelve in an art contest sponsored by the San Gabriel Historical Society and her first one-artist show was held when she was fourteen. Her high school art teacher suggested that she apply for the Saturday Scholarship at the Los Angeles Art Center College of Design; she won the scholarship and began serious art study even before graduating from high school. Later, she was accepted as a full-time student at the Art Center.

Bev graduated in 1968 and was soon married to Jay Doolittle, another art student whom she had met at school. They began married life with a painting trip to Bryce Canyon and Zion National Parks to study and sketch.

For the following five years, the Doolittles worked in art and television production with an advertising agency in Los Angeles. "Initially," says Bev, "my goal was to succeed in the agency world. Jay and I worked together for five years, in the same office and often on the same projects. It was a lot of fun, but at the end of five years, what we were doing in the commercial art world began to be awfully repetitive."

"Jay and I didn't want to live in the city for the rest of our lives. We wanted to be close to nature and we wanted to travel. We took one year and travelled throughout the western United States, Canada and Baja California. We were both trying to find ourselves as artists."

The year-long trip proved to Bev that she had the discipline to work on her own and gave her great inspiration for her art. Since then, the Doolittles have travelled frequently to the wilderness, gathering research material, sketching and photographing for upcoming works. They have camped in Alaska three times, dropped into the wild above the Arctic Circle by a bush pilot. They have trekked through British Columbia, the Rockies and as far away as Tanzania.

Much of Bev's subject matter is provided by the out-of-

Bev sketching on location. Note the similarity in landscape to Season of the Eagle *shown on page 44.*

doors. "I love nature," she says, "I try to look beyond the obvious and create unique, meaningful paintings depicting our Western wilderness and its inhabitants."

Bev Doolittle's art, especially her camouflage work, demands months of development, research of terrain and animals and sketching. After developing the concept, she creates "thumbnail" sketches, up to as many as fifty, where she reworks the image until she has achieved her idea. Next, she works out all the questions of detail in a larger comprehensive pencil drawing. A color study follows, enabling her to determine the colors that add most to the composition. Finally, she decides the size for the original and begins to paint. Her technique is extremely tight and detailed and she works in a very demanding medium – transparent watercolor; it takes long weeks of intensive work to complete an original.

Of her work Bev says, "I start with a concept and attempt to convey it through strong design coupled with detailed realism. I want people to *think* when they look at my paintings."

They do. Bev Doolittle's art compels our involvement. Through the magic of her vision, she forges an interaction between us and her art, rewarding our attention with the excitement of discovery.

Two views of Bev at work in her studio. At left, she is applying color on Guardian Spirits *shown on pages 40 and 41.*

VISIONS: THE ART OF BEV DOOLITTLE

PINTOS

Have you ever noticed that when you walk into a pasture, all the horses raise their heads at once to look at you? I became fascinated with the idea of painting such a scene while observing a small group of chestnut horses. As I worked out the design, I began to think how much fun it would be to have the horses observing you, the viewer, before you saw them. Then, I began to work out ways to camouflage the horses.

The varied abstract markings of pinto horses suggested patterns of snow against rock. The chestnut horses became pintos hidden against a background of sienna-colored rocks and snow patches. The wild pinto ponies all stand alert, already aware of your presence when you discover them.

BUGGED BEAR

Anyone who has ever spent any time in the great north woods knows what a plague the stinging flies and insects can be. Insects bother all animals, not just humans, and the grizzly bear is no exception. The size and strength of the grizzly is no match for the persistent buzz and bite of flying insects. Here, a grizzly lies among a profusion of summer flowers stoically trying to ignore the flies, gnats, bees and mosquitos until their season is over.

WHOO!?

It was ten o'clock at night and still light. My husband Jay and I were sitting quietly beside a campfire at the edge of a small lake in a remote area of northern Canada. It was July and the northern latitude gave us light until eleven p.m. The bush pilot who had flown us there in a small plane had long since left. We were the only people camped around that small, isolated lake, the only people in the whole valley.

You can imagine our surprise at hearing what sounded like a large rock being thrown into the lake. Closer scrutiny revealed that a large beaver slapping his tail on the surface of the lake was the "rock thrower." He was telling us that he was alarmed and displeased at our having camped so close to his home.

The next day, we found his stick and mud lodge along the shore line. On subsequent evenings, we would crouch behind the lodge and take photographs as the beaver family emerged to gather leaves and twigs from a nearby stand of aspen.

Our chance encounter with the beavers led me to wonder about other accidental meetings. I let my sense of fun and whimsy be my guide and Whoo!? is the result.

THE GOOD OMEN

Occasionally while hiking in the desert near my home, I'll get lucky and see a golden eagle. The sight of this magnificent bird soaring free in its environment always inspires me.

The eagle was a source of inspiration for the Native Americans, too. The Indians envisioned the golden eagle as the embodiment of the Great Spirit. By wearing the eagle's feathers, they believed themselves to be possessed of part of the Great Spirit's power. To view a golden eagle while on a raiding or hunting expedition was considered especially lucky.

Here, three Crow Indian warriors watch the silent flight of a golden eagle, probably pausing to give thanks to the Great Spirit for the good omen.

[18]

WOODLAND ENCOUNTER

Woodland Encounter was a challenge I set up for myself. I wanted to do a lot of things at once. First, I wanted to see how far I could take the camouflage idea without losing the image. I wanted to see how many rules I could break and still have the painting work. I wanted to change the experience of seeing. For example, we habitually see the foreground. I wanted to reverse the process and get the viewer to see the background first and the foreground last.

To do that, I decided to place a bright red fox, a target for the eye, in the very center. Of course you're not supposed to center things, but as long as I was breaking rules, I decided to take it a step further. The fox divided the painting in half. I then centered an Indian in the left and right halves. Finally, I chose a landscape that was distracting enough to make discovering the Indians fun for the viewer.

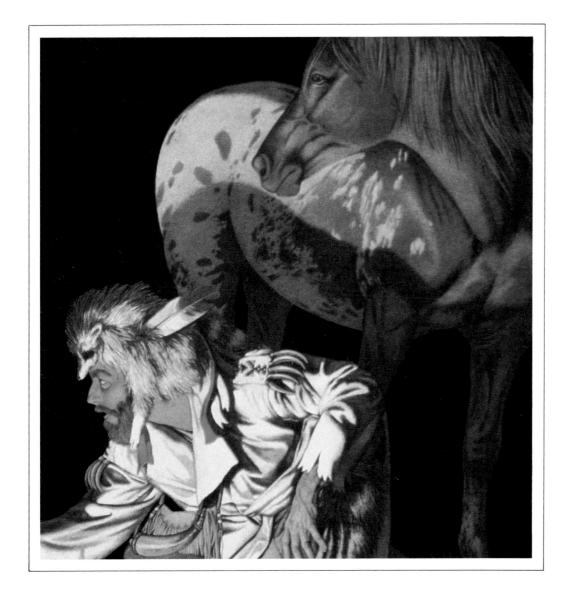

UNKNOWN PRESENCE

If you've ever camped out in the wilderness you can relate to this painting. Picture yourself sitting around a campfire. Somewhere out there in the darkness you hear something. Is it the wind, a bear, or is it just your imagination?

This Mountain Man has heard something and it worries him enough that he's reaching for his rifle. You gotta figure a guy this experienced isn't just imagining things. There really is something out there! If you don't believe him, or me, just look at his horse. He hears it too!

No, I'm not going to tell you what the "Presence" is. I'm not really sure...

SPIRIT OF THE GRIZZLY

The Plains Indian had an intimate knowledge of and a deep respect for the animals that shared his environment. He emulated the courage and hunting skills of many animals and especially coveted the strength of the eagle, buffalo, bear and wolf. By wearing their fur, feathers or claws he hoped to possess a part of their spirit.

This Blackfeet Indian has long studied the mighty grizzly bear. Wrapped in the grizzly's fur, the warrior rides his horse to the edge of a cold mountain stream. We discover he is indeed possessed of the Spirit of the Grizzly.

EAGLE'S FLIGHT

"...through his mane and tail the high wind sings, Fanning the hairs, who wave like feather'd wings."

This line from Shakespeare was the inspiration for Eagle's Flight. *I wanted to portray Shakespeare's words in both a literal and symbolic way.*

I drew the horses in a state of fluid motion to emphasize speed and power. On a symbolic level, I arranged the horses and Indian in such a way that all the "darks" in the painting would create the image of an eagle in flight. The use of eagle feathers as decoration on the horse and rider was also used to emphasize the feeling of flight.

ESCAPE BY A HARE

The components of this scene could all be found right outside my studio window, here in the desert. Breaking the arid expanse of rock and sand are prickly pear cactus and clumps of bunch grass. These have taken on the long shadows of early morning or evening, a very active time of day for the animals who live here.

Black-tailed jack rabbits and red-tailed hawks are common sights.

The red-tail's streaking shadow is more than enough to tell this jack rabbit to run. And that disembodied shadow intensifies our identification with the fleeing jack rabbit.

RUSHING WAR EAGLE

From the time that an Indian is a boy, he seeks to become more and more like the animal he has chosen to be his helper throughout life. When a warrior adorns himself with the eagle's feathers, claws, and bones, he brings to himself the special strengths and abilities of the great Eagle Spirit. Rushing War Eagle is a painting of a warrior who has been empowered by his chosen protector — the golden eagle.

RUNS WITH THUNDER

To the Plains Indian the buffalo meant life. The buffalo provided almost everything necessary to the Indian's daily life — food, clothing, and shelter. It was no wonder the buffalo was so highly revered.

This Sioux warrior has chosen the buffalo as his Spirit protector and supernatural helper.

The sounds of thunder and the thundering hooves of a herd of buffalo are apt to sound alike. It seemed appropriate to visually relate buffalo with thunder. This similarity became the inspiration for both the Indian's name and the title of this painting.

[28]

CHRISTMAS DAY, GIVE OR TAKE A WEEK

After the giant Sequoias were established as a National Park in 1890, Congress also designated the "General Grant" tree as the Nation's Christmas tree. How appropriate with the cinnamon-red bark and "Christmas" green foliage against a backdrop of "snow-white" snow.

As much as I would have liked to paint the "General Grant" tree — it just didn't have a very good cave. So I made up my very own "Christmas Sequoia" for this mountain man to find shelter, peace, and warmth in on Christmas Day. He has unloaded his horse, gathered wood, made a fire, and has rigged up a makeshift cooking stick for his meal of a local game bird. He has even taken time to cut down a small tree and decorate it with his meager possessions — a locket, a pocket watch, an Indian shell necklace, and a mirror.

I would imagine the mountain man's calendar was not too accurate, therefore I've decided to title this painting, Christmas Day, Give or Take a Week.

LET MY SPIRIT SOAR

There is something so peaceful about the quiet gaze of a day dreamer! It seems to me to be a very mystical state. The Plains Indians had a very profound connection to the mystical world. In their daydreams; there must have been a magical, unbounded quality.

Let My Spirit Soar portrays a young Blackfoot woman who has come to her favorite sunny place to reflect and to dream. The flock of white birds reflected in the water beside her are symbols of her spirit's purity and freedom.

THE FOREST HAS EYES

A solitary mountain man guides his mount through the shallows of a stream. Leading a pack horse, he enters the territory of hostile Indians. A feeling of apprehension, a sense of foreboding, sweep over him. He studies the trees as they grow more dense and press even closer. It's as though The Forest Has Eyes.

I want the viewer to share the emotions of the rider, and like him, be able to study the detail of each leaf and every branch that surrounds him. Soon, it may become apparent that the forest has eyes, and the eyes have faces.

This is my finest camouflage to date. I've compromised nothing. It's the most ambitious piece I've undertaken. The picture is the product of years of experience and planning, and has taken more than six months of intensive painting.

WOLVES OF THE CROW

To be like a wolf was not a role undertaken lightly by any Crow warrior. The special qualities of wolves — endurance, loyalty and tracking ability — made the warriors who took their power from the wolf esteemed members of the tribe. Being like a wolf meant studying the ways and habits of wolves, focusing one's energies on living the way of the wolf. Such single-minded diligence led to great skills, ensuring the tribe's survival.

Wolves of the Crow is a painting of Crow Indian warriors who have attained the honor of scout. Wearing the sacred wolf skin, the scouts can call upon the prowess of wolf spirits to help them in the hunt.

TWO INDIAN HORSES

It's Fall, 1875. A regiment of the Second Cavalry takes a short reconnaissance ride from Fort Ellis, Montana. The soldiers have stopped to rest the horses and themselves before moving on to complete the last of many such rides before the onset of winter.

When I design a painting I try to guide the viewer's eye to points within the picture that best communicate my story. The sequence in which the viewer discovers elements in a painting is planned. It is my hope that most people will experience the painting to its best possible level.

As a rule, most people view things from left to right…it's a habit from reading. So, by camouflaging the two Blackfeet Indians, it is my hope that the viewer will pass over the Indians on the extreme left of the painting, continue on down the row of horses to the soldier walking off the extreme right end of the painting. By having most of the horses turned and looking off to the right helps to subtly force the viewer's eye to the right and away from the "discovery" of the Indians. Discovering the Indians last rather than first helps to make the story more believable and lots more fun. These Blackfeet Indians are about to be two horses richer, hence the title, Two Indian Horses.

[37]

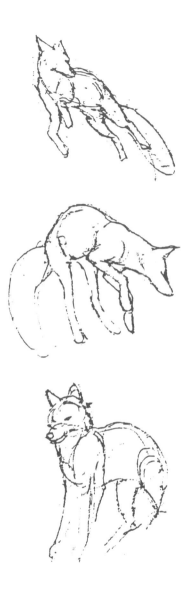

MISSED

Camouflaging the arrow was the key here. I purposely made the arrow difficult to see at first glance. You have to work a little to get the key to the puzzle. Once you see it, the story is waiting for you. For myself, I think the arrow was shot by a young boy. Most warriors would hunt bigger game. But I don't think we'll ever know for sure.

TWO BEARS OF THE BLACKFEET

The lives of the Blackfeet Indians were full of danger and uncertainty. Surrounded by a harsh world where attacks by animals or hostile tribes, sickness and starvation were ever-present threats, they relied on the spirit world for protection.

For the Plains Indians, the grizzly bear was second only to the buffalo in his supernatural powers. The bear was revered for his strength, agility, vitality and invulnerability to arrows, bullets and other animals. He was also believed to possess great wisdom and the ability to find herbs to heal his wounds.

The Blackfeet warrior Two Bears received the powers of the grizzly in his vision quest. His vision spirit instructed him on the contents of his "medicine bundle," an important symbol of his powers. Two Bears has studied and emulated the ways of the grizzly and has become a mighty and bear-like warrior, respected and feared by his enemies.

[39]

GUARDIAN SPIRITS

A solitary Blackfeet warrior rides across the snow-covered wilderness. But he is not alone. His spear, his shield and his clothing are all adorned with the pelts and feathers of the fiercest predators in his land. Through a dream quest, the warrior has earned the spiritual protection of the animals that he admires for their ferocity and cunning. They warn him of danger, increase his battle prowess and give him magical strength.

Wolf-brother, symbol of stamina and hunting prowess, makes up his headress. The wolf was messenger and guide to the spirit world. He can warn the warrior of danger and the whereabouts of enemies. The Great Bear, venerated for wisdom and strength, is his shield. The bear was invulnerable to most arrows and bullets, and he could heal himself or restore life to those he especially favored. The Weasel, whose pelt decorates the warrior's sleeves, was respected as a fierce fighter and represented "good war medicine." The mountain lion spirit in his riding cloth gives him ferocity and independence, while the eagle feathers on his headress lend him speed and contact with the Great Spirit. With their powerful protection, he need fear no enemy, be it man, beast or spirit.

CALLING THE BUFFALO

In Calling the Buffalo, *a medicine man of the Sioux has been chosen by his tribe to call the great herd. He goes away from his camp, choosing one of the infrequent water holes from which to make his prayers. Guided by rituals handed down from the medicine men of one generation to another, he chants and prays to the spirit of the buffalo. He uses the powerful magic of a buffalo skull to entice the herd into this tribe's territory. Knowing his people's survival depends upon his success, he focuses his spiritual power and casts his big medicine into his call. The only question remaining is, will the buffalo heed his call?*

SEASON OF THE EAGLE

In the life of the Indian, every new day, every encounter with bird or beast, and everything he owned or wore had religious significance. The Indians prayed each day to the One-Who-Made-All-Things, the Crow Ah-badt-dadt-deah. Since all creatures were made by the Great Spirit, the Indian considered the animals and birds with whom he shared his home not only sacred, but brothers. Each creature had unique powers and skills and the Indians believed that God had placed them on the Mother Earth to teach them valuable lessons.

The eagle embodied courage and speed, skills the Indians needed for successful war and hunting, and eagles were revered as messengers of the Great Spirit.

In the highest passes of the Rocky Mountains, spring arrives late in the year. As the snow melts, swollen, rushing streams and rivers tell the Indians that passes to more fertile hunting grounds will be open. The melting snow patterns speak to the Indians also. These are messages from the Great Spirit.

It is because of the Indians' special reverence for the eagle that I have chosen to incorporate him into my most recent painting, Season Of The Eagle.

DOUBLED BACK

For me, the grizzly bear is a very special animal. His presence adds an excitement that no other North American animal can match.

I've created this painting to share the sense of excitement I feel in grizzly country. The setting is a small mountain valley where the remnant snow

patches clearly show the tracks of a large grizzly. How long has it been since he was standing right here...where is he now? Look closely at those tracks. The snow is crisp and the edges haven't begun to melt yet. These grizzly tracks are fresh. How far ahead is he? Not far, not far at all...

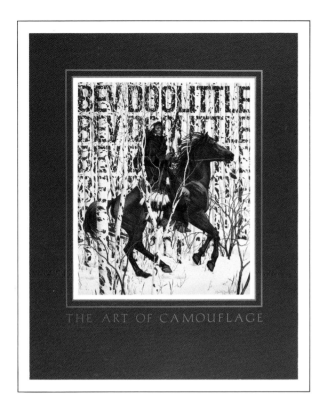

ART OF CAMOUFLAGE

The challenge here was to use camouflage art in a new way; incorporating words into the design. I did a series of backgrounds, different kinds of rocks and trees. Once I had ironed out the concept, I settled down and had fun. An Indian warrior on horseback is one of my favorite subjects to paint.

WHERE SILENCE SPEAKS: THE ART OF BEV DOOLITTLE

Where Silence Speaks: The Art of Bev Doolittle *was conceived in the tradition of the great French art books of the Fifteenth Century. Published as a limited edition, it is not just a book, but also an unique work of art incorporating the work of Bev Doolittle, poetry and prose by Elise Maclay and design by Peter Landa. Sixteen images are reproduced in eight colors on custom-formulated paper. Left unbound, they are fitted into a hand-made portfolio, which is lined on the inside with a ribbon-tied velour chemise. The portfolio is then housed in a gold-stamped solander box. Accompanied by the limited edition print* Missed.

LIST OF PUBLISHED WORKS

Title	Year Published	Edition Size	Issue Price (U.S.)
PINTOS	1979	1,000	$65
THE GOOD OMEN	1980	1,000	$85
BUGGED BEAR	1980	1,000	$85
WHOO!?	1980	1,000	$75
WOODLAND ENCOUNTER	1981	1,500	$145
UNKNOWN PRESENCE	1981	1,500	$135
SPIRIT OF THE GRIZZLY	1981	1,500	$150
EAGLE'S FLIGHT	1982	1,500	$185
ESCAPE BY A HARE (Cameo)	1983	1,500	$80
RUSHING WAR EAGLE	1983	1,500	$150
ART OF CAMOUFLAGE (Signed Poster)	1983	2,000	$55
ART OF CAMOUFLAGE (Unsigned Poster)	1983	2,000	$40
RUNS WITH THUNDER	1983	1,500	$150
CHRISTMAS DAY, GIVE OR TAKE A WEEK (Personal Commission)	1983	4,581	$80
LET MY SPIRIT SOAR	1984	1,500	$195
THE FOREST HAS EYES (Personal Commission)	1984	8,544	$175
WOLVES OF THE CROW	1985	2,650	$225
TWO INDIAN HORSES (Personal Commission)	1985	12,253	$225
MISSED (Accompanied Limited Edition Book)	1986	3,500	
WHERE SILENCE SPEAKS: THE ART OF BEV DOOLITTLE (Limited Edition Book – Livre De Luxe)	1986	3,500	$650
TWO BEARS OF THE BLACKFEET	1986	2,650	$225
GUARDIAN SPIRITS (Personal Commission)	1987	13,238	$295
CALLING THE BUFFALO	1987	8,500	$245
SEASON OF THE EAGLE (Personal Commission)	1988	36,548	$245
DOUBLED BACK	1988	15,000	$245

THE LIMITED EDITION PRINT

FOR THE PAST fifteen years, The Greenwich Workshop has been one of the leading publishers of fine art limited edition prints.

Limited edition signed and numbered collector prints are a relatively recent development in the art world. They are top quality reproductions of an artist's original work. When an edition is limited, it means that a predetermined number of prints are produced. Each print in the edition is signed by the artist and consecutively numbered. The artist's signature assures that the reproduction is faithful to the original art and the numbering assures the strictly limited edition size. Upon completion of an edition, all production plates and film are destroyed – a final assurance to the collector that the image will never again be reproduced as a fine art print.

In recent years, sophisticated printing technology has advanced to the point where offset printing utilizing laser scanning, dry trapping and add-on colors has enabled us to produce facsimile reproductions that mirror an artist's original work.

The Greenwich Workshop's prints are known not only for their fidelity to the original artwork but also for their quality. They are produced with painstaking attention to detail and color, with the artist, printing specialists and The Greenwich Workshop working together over a period of months to develop and perfect the finished print.

The Greenwich Workshop's commitment is to quality; to the production of the finest limited edition prints, prints of works by fine artists like Bev Doolittle, prints which will be treasured for generations to come.